What a lovely ruthless and tender book this is! In the subtly-titled *Where Do the Memories Go?* Lauri Robertson tracks the path of her inner life as it meets the realities of the outer world, unflinching under the impacts of loss, grief, pain, death and the fear of death where she finds, or does not find, the needed words. A powerful centerpiece to the book, "The Grievous Body," articulates the scenes of an unspoken farewell to her dying mother-in-law and meditates on them. The elegy "For Dori," honoring a beloved friend, raises challenging questions for the poet herself: "in my heart, my aging heart, how inaccessible the story of being or not." Yet poetry enables these stories to end both ways: "I love … every blistered apocryphal moment, /as tho' to breathe were life" and "Just say/ she died." To read this book is to join in understanding these ancient and sustaining truths.
    Jane Augustine

Lauri Robertson's poems are morsels to savor. She shares Proustian madeleines—hers, in a small crystal wine glass, just big enough for "a splash", that takes her back to her father. You walk with her through her garden of *fleurs sauvages*, run your fingers over the stone crevices of the French medieval village walls, eavesdrop on her conversations, with her mother, maybe with you, with all of us, lucky enough to listen. These poems, and especially those on memory, are nothing short of the most profound philosophical meditations on living, loving, losing, and growing old.
    Nancy Sherman

Listen. Put your ear to the door and you will overhear whispers, laughter, prayers and protests, wry observations and revelations from a mind trained to listen and follow the twisting paths of words. Lauri Robertson's poems in these companion volumes—*In Concert* and *Where Do the Memories Go?*—inscribe worlds. We turn the pages, encounter story after story. Every poem an image, a plot, mysterious and tangible. Loss, love, rage, solitude, self and memory, sentiment, the salve of creativity— our human lexicon—tendered by a feeling mind by turns wry, humorous, provoking, inflected with wisdom and curiosity—always honest. Nothing seems to come between Robertson and the page; she trusts it utterly and is wholly herself. Hers is a voice we want to hear.
    Anne Troutman

Where Do the Memories Go?
Lauri Robertson

Spuyten Duyvil
New York City

© 2021 Lauri Robertson
ISBN 978-1-952419-74-4
Cover photo by the author: "The Duck Pond" 2012

Library of Congress Cataloging-in-Publication Data

Names: Robertson, Lauri Rosemary, author.
Title: Where do the memories go? / Lauri Robertson.
Description: New York City : Spuyten Duyvil, [2021] |
Identifiers: LCCN 2021020260 | ISBN 9781952419744 (paperback)
Subjects: LCGFT: Poetry.
Classification: LCC PS3618.O316978 W47 2021 | DDC 811/.6--dc23
LC record available at https://lccn.loc.gov/2021020260

for Julie (1932-2018)

Where Do the Memories Go?

Contents

I
All Faces Grow Old 3
You May Want 5
Ephemera 7
Old Women 10
Generational 11
The Old Stone House 12
Mirror 13

II
Death of the French Doctor 19
The Priest is Weary 23
for Anthony Bourdain 24
The Catalpa Trees 26
This is What Memory Is 27
for Dori Laub 29
Keeping the Dead Alive 30

III
The Grievous Body 37
  1-8

IV
The Old Abbaye 51
In the Shadow of the Imaginable 52
The Real People 54
Finding a Mantra 56
Stigma 58
Bounties 59
My Father's Wine Glasses 60
1950's 62
Why the Old Look Backwards 65

V

Persona Poem 71
In The Catacombs 73
for Emily 75
Hospital 77
It's Not Death 79
The C Word 80
The End of Immortality 83
Arc 85

I

All Faces Grow Old

All faces grow old alike.
You say, *no*, some are more
beautiful still.
But, wait long enough
and they're all the same —
old, old, old.

What is that quality
time alone wreaks?
Nice for furniture, sometimes
or trees, often, for stone
waiting millennia to crumble.

What is it about keeping
or trying to keep
what's not yet lost?
(Or, is it?)

A face means so little
and so much — what others
see, but we can't quite —
faceless in the great
planetary blur of many.
(So, so many.)

I told a friend, to quell anxiety
I think of how unimportant
one is in the grand scheme.
"Does it help?" she asked.
"No," I said, "It just makes me feel
small and inconsequential."

All faces, unique as snowflakes
are nevertheless recognizable.
Everyone resembles someone
from some century.

Perhaps beneath Paris
your doppelgänger
is illuminating the catacombs
like tracery or fretwork
beautiful and burnished.

When I was young I wanted to look
like no one, invisible, myself, a self
that couldn't be set in time or place
primitive yet civilized, unadorned
but for a shard of antiquity.

You May Want

You may want to start
thinking about regret
in the future tense.
(I'd say, *have* to start
but don't like to bully
anyone.)

One day regret will become
what you didn't want
to die without

seeing, doing, having, being.

(Of course, there're no regrets
if you're actually dead.)

So, now you'll tell me
that sounds like a "bucket list"
and it is, well

not one of those travelogues
"50 Places to See Before You Die"
something more spectral, something

you may reach for with your arms
till they showed the banjo strings
(to quote Robert Frost)

perhaps not longing at all
but its absence, days
in abeyance, *chuchotement*.

Yes, I'd like to see
Mount-Saint-Michel
who wouldn't?

But, more than that
or just as much, ride the train
to such a destination, looking

out the window at far fields
or a blur of all, and none.
(*What are all those fuzzy looking things out there?*)

…regret I hadn't come
to a place where ambition
means nothing, indecision
means nothing, resentment
bitterness, tacit sorrow, regret
mean nothing, where Lear says

Nothing will come of nothing
and you do not have to
speak again.

Ephemera

Why is it all
ephemeral? Why
does it all have to be
ephemeral?

Weeds from the secret garden
I choose to call flowers
'sauvages de ma rue'
et tu Brute? Ephemeral
all

and quotidian, even boring
until we do not exist.

Then you're an absence — *absence*
as in the particular kind of seizure
in which no arms are flung.
You're just missing
for a few seconds
or missed.

But, remarkably dependable
(Should I depend on anything?)
the weird and motley
extravagance of *fleurs*
whether I can keep up with them
or not, keep coming.

*

As the chapters close, they fold
like a very special kind of origami
leaves collapsing onto themselves
in every imaginable configuration

folded and torn like deckle
cut cleanly as an umbilical cord
too many images, too many
metaphors, trying too hard.

In feeling less useful (useless?)
use comes, scaffolding of purpose
resignation, a last glimpse.
My goddess, I still have eyes!

*

And, so I was here.
I have a photograph
worth a thousand words
to have and to hold
to devour, as if one could —
a world beyond beauty
(that difficult, silly thing)
a place where a lens holds
our lives like a bookmark
miraculously, stopping time
begging for memories
of what never occurred
but were skin and flame
felt and cherished
beyond evanescence.

On what path should I step
being an old woman
for a visual thrill
for moss and woodpiles
woodpiles covered with moss.
I've seen them, and become them
radiating green to yellow
embraced by stone.

What is time but what
alone does this?

Sentiment moves
elsewhere.
It's entirely fictional
of course
like falling in and out
of love

a room
in which I want to live
here not there
despite all obstacles
what sounds good or reasonable
fantasy or phantasy
whatever was made up
from a picture —

no illusion, illusion
is only imagining.

Old Women

How perverse it was to see
old women with big rings.

But, now I understand the utility
of slightly gaudy jewelry.

A young woman with a dot
or a dash, however uncertain

or deprived
bespeaks fresh flesh.

Gold bangles, antique perhaps
or semi-precious encrusted

gifts hold their own
on a spotted arm.

I have had, and I have won.
I'm going to my grave

neither poor nor unloved
unancestored or unaccessorized.

They say you can't
take it with you.

Don't look at me, look
at what I take with me.

Generational

All I really want to do, is, baby
live my little life with you.
The smaller the better.

We can read and write, figure out
what to cook each day or two
watch a movie now and then

stroll, and see the world
collapsing in the distance, our own
shallow importances, shallower still.

But, *Oh* that moment when
the hot water hits, the ineluctable sigh
echoing from long and

more than a few others ago
the silken warmth of sliding into bed
as two, traversing the universe.

All I really want is *what?*
Isn't it silly, I can't think of anything.
Clay and wattles.

We turn it over to the next
because we don't want it any more
if we ever did, or

our grasp weakens, remits.
We know they think they can do better.
We wish they could.

Old Stone House

Some things were here
before you came
and some will be long after.

Good to recognize which
and that nothing is forever —
St. Malo, younger than my mother.

Maybe it will moss and craze.
Salvage the soot of Bordeaux
and there you go.

Revision by century — who
regrets Haussmann's Paris
or dares to say out loud?

Some things will not need fixing
for another few decades
so why bother?

What year were you born?
Leave it alone!

Mirror

I look in the mirror and see
my parents, in turn
my father and mother
mother and father
thinking of each
conjuring them
thinking

I'm no more responsible
for my character
than I am
for my face.

Mirror

I look in the mirror and see
my parents in me
my father and mother
brother and sister
something of each
comparing them
thinking

I am far more responsible
for my character
than I am
for my face

II

II

Death of the French Doctor

I can write this, and no one will know
what I'm talking about, or whom.
No privacy intruded upon, only
a skeleton of fact beneath fantasy.

I think of my sister-in-law
speaking of my mother-in-law's death
(which we knew would come
but weren't nearly prepared for).

"Where do all the memories go?" she asked.
Some, passed along, archive and history
but, every sentient, corporeal thought
particular and fleeting, even to the rememberer?

Every peaceful, lonely moment of being
my flesh, my breath.

*

I'd seen him twice
once with my husband
who is a bit complicated
and needed good care.

I listened with my own eyes.
(A foreigner lives in mixed metaphors.)
He was smart. I told him
he was very kind, which indeed
he seemed, a serious, gentle
country doctor.

But, he'd have nothing to do
with being buttered up
in bad, sycophantic French.
"*C'est normale.*" he said, rather rudely.

The next time, I arrived with a translation.
"What do you want?" he said
in perfect English, none too nicely.
I pointed to the note in front of him.

He softened after looking in my ear
the drum doubtless cloudy, perhaps bulging.
He tried to help me pronounce
I forget what word.

*

How can he be dead —
he belonged here — and I
a stranger, am still alive?

He was a doctor and
as we know, they're
supposed to be immortal.

We could all say, *it was his time*
as if we knew what time that was
or what time is, as if
a body could tell time.

But, this man, this citizen
of this village, even an outsider
could see it wasn't nearly his
even as the sun setting didn't lie.

Forgive us our counting and planning
or foolish, useless providence.
Give us belonging

good deeds lasting

the handwritten prescription
for my feverish ear
my longing to win him
and confide.

He is as mourned as he was mortal.

Let *me* belong here, if not by birth
then by rooftops. If not by language
then evening light.

Let us all belong
by nature, and choice.

      *

Cher Docteur dans la rivière
Dear Doctor in the river, in practice
for 38 years down the street
with 6, he told me, to go.
I tried to convince him to accept us
earnest, decent folks
lovers of old stone.

But, you may want, and have
to tell a story many times
to get it, not right, but full
not true, but fully shaded:

Actually, I later learned
he wasn't all that well liked.
Some, apparently, found him brusque
and there were unflattering stories
about wives and mistresses.
(I wasn't paying full attention or
more likely, didn't follow the French.)

There were speculations
about his disappearance
which I won't share.
But even I, more bewildered
than bereaved, imagined
he just wanted to escape
and is alive.

The Priest is Weary

There was a fancy wedding this evening
at the church in the square, half the men in tails.
I saw him leaving just after, solitary of course
by medieval formality —

God's bridegroom, black gown fluttering
around his bicycle.

Parishes are too small for a priest of their own
so he runs between several, like a country doctor
(of whom there are also too, exhausted, few).

Today's resplendent wedding
had several hundred, replete with silk
feathers and lace, the young couple
privileged indeed. But, immodest
in the eyes of the villagers or *noblesse oblige*
we know life isn't usually easy.

On Monday, it will be a funeral.
I happen to know her, an old woman
a fixture behind French doors
in the other square, in her nightgown
with her cigarette, and stringy hair.

Her death caused little disruption
or surprise. Her daughter, perhaps
bereaved as much by her life.

I liked her though, my own mother
not so dissimilar. We happened to share
a love of stray cats, in fact, a cat.

The weary priest will be there.

for Anthony Bourdain (1956-2018)

Being wisely in pain
is no solution, none at all.
Why couldn't you just have died
of something *normal* — a heart attack
for example, or in a plane crash?

And not leave a sad world
to speculate, or rail against French wine
(OK, I get it, *dangereuse*), or possibly
a possibly punctured romance.
Hard judgments all around.

We actually went to college together
although I didn't know you.
But, *Tony, why didn't you call me?*

It's not that we thought
(or I thought) you had it all together.
Not that I even liked every bit of shtick.
Your energy seemed high risk
but I'd hoped it was theater.

Sorry for your pain, and sorrier
for the child's pain.
Sorry for a painful world
you softened until stunning
and leaving the rest of us
bewildered, for a moment
wondering, *Where else is there
to go?*

*

He became a kind of Rorschach
for the world.

He died
of a broken heart
stone cold sober.

Black Widow Psycho-Bitch
killed him.

Addicts can't drink.
Alcohol killed him.
Fame killed him.
Fatigue killed him.

Boredom killed him.
Branding killed him.

Bipolar II Disorder
Attention Deficit Hyperactivity Disorder
killed him.

Existential Despair
nowhere to go but down
killed him.

A dozen wacky conspiracy theories
killed him.

The Catalpa Trees

We always worry about them
even knowing they'll be late.

Ornamental with long, thin beans
swaying like Victoriana.

Catalpa, an unusual name
not easily forgotten.

I look at it for the first time now
made up of *cat,* my dearest creature
of course memorable.

One in the neighbor's yard — summer people —
another across the street, stately and spindly
covered with lichen, baleful for trees.

In April and May others flourish
Kwanzan cherries and Bradford pears
those standard, suburban-looking things.

But, the catalpa trees are bare
corpse-like as trees can be
dead for sure this year.

I say this knowing, of course, that's not the case.
It never is. They're just late.

But, stunned, I've neglected to say
to remember until this exact moment
our neighbor won't be here.

He is not late. He is now bare.

This is What Memory Is

I am in France buying salmon
and see the word *saumon*
say it out loud, and think
of my friend ordering dinner.
She was German. She said
the English with a 'Z'
and tiniest bit of 'l' — *Zalmon*.
My Zalmon.

Her lovely, lilting accent —
percipient reprieve from guttural?
Her whole life story as I know it
a shallow, imagined version.
Her version gone — memory
not everlasting.

Zalmon — neither nostalgia nor
mawkish sentiment, but bringing
to whatever mind is left
the imprint of her everything
a post-war German woman
who had to live with being that.

A graceful woman, fearless
beyond my shallow imagining
of living a new life, an ordinary life
among us, as if life could ever be
ordinary. *My Zalmon is lovely!*

We were happy to be
in a nice restaurant, in
the city where she had to stay
near the hospital, away
from her American dog
and husband who never
became American. This

is memory, 'triggered' and cued
simple, redundant, redux?
A fractal of synapse, love
her husband gone now, too.

This is memory, claim
and hold it, cherish each
morsel, embellishment.
Why?

for Dori Laub (1937-2018)

We will be dust with you, Dori.
We'll follow you, brightly
colored shoes, or not
with memories and sorrows
anyone to remember us
or not, we will follow.
Beloved, cherished says poetry
of the grave, but in my heart
my aging heart, truly
beloved, and cherished.
I imagine time passing because
it's normal, and yet how strange
how inaccessible the story
of being and not. *Being*
goes with a name we're given
the naming itself
more abstract, yes
the breath, *Hashem*
ineffable.

Keeping the Dead Alive

Every sense of them, yes
but certain things, the shape
of fingernails, toenails, too.
Tell me I'm not wrong.

Where do the memories go? —
my sister-in-law's perhaps
inadvertently philosophical question.
A religious question?

Even atheists believe
in religious *feeling*
but truly I believe
it all just disappears.

Ossuary, crematory, periodic table
of the elements.

But, they're 'alive'
because we loved them
or didn't even, but knew them.
After great pain, sometimes
it's just a puzzle, unsolvable
by the arrogance of philosophy
religion, too. Don't get me started…

But, I loved them, especially
at this moment, visiting Bill's city
picturing his elegant hand
holding a perfectly sharpened pencil
to write a chemical formula
on faded blue paper
a vision so fresh it could
hardly be called *memory*.

III

III

The Grievous Body

This is thy hour O Soul, thy free flight into the wordless...
— Walt Whitman

1

How quickly you do not look
like yourself. The body
uninhabited, unnamed
now just, *the corpse*.
Death is so generic

and instructive. Now, even *we*
are dying, our generation, our friends
suddenly, as happens sometimes
preternaturally, prematurely.
We should be so lucky
as to fear growing old.

Lying down after gardening
or because he felt ill
his face changed, morphed
into a waxy, unrecognizable
version of itself.

I've heard this happens
very quickly, nothing like
the beautiful marble effigies
of nobles and saints.

Even after long nearing
thinner and thinner, an artificial
slumber, sallow, and prophesied.

Now, I have to think of them
differently.

Everyone you knew, or who
loved the sorrows of your changing face
has to think of you
very differently.

Leave me alone now.
I want to feel sad.
I meet with bitter alacrity
the grievous body.

2

Bizarre as it is
a mawkish Hollywood trope
I kid you not

in a snazzy assisted-living complex
complete with beauty parlor
and ceramics studio (sign me up!)
vultures assemble on the rooftops.

Which building they choose
depends. They shuffle around
a vulturine committee.

Beautiful birds in flight
they could almost be eagles
(Yes, please assist me with living!)
until you see their mercenary eyes
demonic red faces.

They don't hurt anyone.
They don't kill anything
those birds of a feather.

But, they choose the roof.
How could it not be?
Bizarrely, they choose the roof.

    3

I think of her when I'm ill
the way she lay down
promptly, somewhat twisted
and to the left.

When I'm ill I think of her
the last curvature
of the crescent moon
incandescent as we all have been
at birth's cry.

What relief those first
moments of touching down
solace of a soft surface
and for the weariness
that refuses to suspect.

I think of her
a bodily memory
of gesture, sharper
than anything
actually remembered.

I used to joke
I married my husband
for his mother — not entirely
untrue.

And, I think of the future
far into it, I hope
(How far can it be?)
when I will curl
too.

4

She tried to get ready
for a long time, for years
the hemlock in a safe place
"A Clear Midnight" covertly
taped inside a kitchen cabinet.

She tried to be ready
and thought she was.
But, more and more
she was afraid, or worse
and the small world
was still bright. She liked
to watch the songbirds
outside.

When I told her I loved
Chenonceau, she pulled out her ticket
from 40 years ago. How wonderful
devotion, *dévouement*
cherishing, *chérir.*

5

It started to become time to say goodbye
though we didn't say it. Or said
in small fragments, both we and she
knowing. It was time. We knew
it would soon be time. And yet
we were unprepared. The very state
of being prepared became normal
and left us stunned.

"Am I going to die today?" she asked.
When my wits returned, I said
Do you want to die today?
"No, not particularly." she replied.
Good, then let's not.

There was a moment I believe
she knew. Her granddaughter
across the room
had been encouraged
to move to the bedside.

Her eyes flashed a look
of extraordinary patience
and strange, almost pity.

She was as ready
as one can never be.
She wasn't ready but
the grievous body was.

6

Last hours
it becomes

not, it
becomes *never*
wisp

body of bird bones
and bruises
beating breath

the last
lucid or terrified
trace of a smile.

The wind
however much you lean into it
turns you away.

Even extraordinary women wear out.
Dare I be diminished?

The 'soul' really does leave —
all that was thought, everyone
who was loved

each cherished object
on the shelf:

*Who's the child in that photograph
from another century?*

"She's my grandmother."

A collection of pitchers
from which to pour water
or milk.

Outside, there's a storm
like a chorus of songbirds
crickets like a chorus
of feral cats.

Do not hasten
to hasten.

Age is dust.

7

At times, she became terrified
they were trying to kill her.

After the last fall and fracture
delirium, "H" became *hospice*
not *hospital,* comfort care
their little cocktail. I asked
"Where do you draw the line?"
"We don't." they said.

Goodbye to the light
last *respite of breath*
the pain which remains
the new world
of the unfortunate body
the longing only to be soothed.

When I told her I loved her
she smiled, and sighed.

Goodbye to the ecstatic light.

The night watch seemed
interminable. Each of us went
crazy in our own way, or not
the eyedropper, surreptitious.
It was right. Please

do it for me.

8

There are archivists
so that no little piece
of life is lost. Although
all are, of course, eventually
if not already, what the photograph
didn't frame, before or after
the thought too fleeting
to entwine. Or, someone else's
memory, pressed like a fern
in an unread book.

Where do the memories go?
I keep asking, over and over
or looking for them, trying
to remember hers when I
can barely remember my own.

They go nowhere.
Press the fern to your lips
or into wet clay.

Or, they dull, or embellish.
What of them lasts, in what form?
Meaning? Must there be?
Regret, maybe?

I remembered
there's such a thing
as 'stinging nettle'.
I looked it up and
sure enough, there it was
and had stung beyond promise.

Our neighbor went
to an interment yesterday
in a country not her own.
She wrote a reminiscence
in a language not her own
read by the son of the dead
to share that shapeless
indefatigable thing.

IV

VI

The Old Abbaye

There used to be geese
a quintet that swam in unison
and goats with Rastafarian coats
a very old horse.
I loved him.

The old abbaye is now a school
as it was centuries ago.
I like the students, noisy
with their red sweaters
and soccer balls.

And the priests
in their handsome inky cassocks
shimmering like the abundant blackbirds
and crows in the neighborhood.
I feel their longing for God
beyond abstraction.

We hear there are nuns, too
but haven't seen them.
Cloistered, I imagine, also in black.
I can feel their invisibility
a trick of bats at night
their witchy, satiated
longing.

Humility, divinity, grace.
I miss the goats.

In the Shadow of the Imaginable

From an upper window
I watch the school children
walking down the street —
in twos mostly, boys first
then the girls, perhaps the teachers
organized it that way.
I think they're 9 or 10
for sure before the bloom.

I remember being that age
on the occasional school trip
being herded, slightly unruly
tall, short, thin, fat, chatting
a skip now and then
unselfconscious.

And, I think of the shadow
I lived under
equally unselfconsciously.
Really, we didn't really know
color or money or status
humiliation or rage, shame.
We were all just *middle class*.
(America had a middle class
back then.)

It was always part of the story
my grandmother committed suicide
or, less fancily, killed herself.
It was long before I was born
almost before my mother was born —
a five year old who went on
to her own madnesses.

There were consequences —
memories I hold now
into old age, sharp as banality.
I'll tell you sometime...

But, what I remember today
and hear in the little hoof beats
ascending from the street:

The weight of the shadow
is there, but not really extant
in school children. What's known
is known without meaning
though that will come, the story
lived, somehow plainer, more
'normal' than it will later sound.

Innocence does not
blame or fear or question itself
nor curtail blithe skipping.

Tragedy is unimaginable
even as the story is one's own.

The Real People

I've always loved
the real people
but knew I could never
be one.

By nature or nurture
or both, I was destined
to be an archivist
an appreciative one

whose cheer might be
time to ponder.

We come in all different
stars and stripes
full of love, I hope
but, a realist, sadly concluding
the sorrowful exists
in abundance.

So, who are they?

I used to ride the bus
way up town. They
seemed real there.
Because there was poverty
that no one would want
to feign? Or, that I was poorer
in ways it would take
a lifetime to respect.

I used to call myself a
descendant of Polish peasants
but didn't realize Jews
had a different meme
I also didn't have.

Identity politics requires identity.

I was a strangely displaced
citizen of the world, member
of a tribe, I thought, of kindness
and ethical belief.

Fucking dreamers!

Who in this world
is to blame for what —
avarice, sloth, the Industrial Revolution
smog in London, Dickensian orphans —
All so long ago, so what?

Now, *authenticity* has become
an obnoxious word. Guess what
it's not that *fill in the blank*
isn't real, it's just that it really is
vacuous, toxic, greedy
fill in the blank!

Like nostalgia for the suburbs
(which have always depressed
the shit out of me!).

Finding a Mantra

Well, I don't know a thing
about it, but a friend or two
said it would be relaxing.
One was going teach me.
"But, I can't give you a mantra."
As I said, I don't know anything, but
thought I'd choose my own.

(Perhaps that's not allowed, but
I didn't want to look it up.
How tacky can an American
fakeoid meditator-to-be be?)

Streams of words flowed
into rivers of possibility.
It should be something
unemotional, maybe. But
meaningful, in my imagination
meditative. Not a recently dead pet
but one long gone, of childhood
the past perfect.

OK, I know it's supposed to be
a secret. OK, I'll tell you
Cleo, short for Cleopatra.

What more is there to say?
A spaniel mutt, blue-black
as the ripest blackberries
and twice as sweet.

(There was a dog, but
were there parents?
The past was not perfect
and now I'm sad.)

I can't remember her
well enough, just her little
doggie face, or is that
a memory of a photograph?

Just when she had medicine
that turned her urine purple
before we had to take her in.

(Why do you need to know this?
Why is sorrow encoded in
the subtlest bits?)

Just a black dog, shiny and wavy
just that I loved her
and that was enough.

Stigma

Please understand, drama fades
even yours, even the most
charred history, or that which maimed
out of ordinary misfortune, neglect.

I wanted to be a warrior, a warrior
filled with love, but was merely
frightened, terrified actually
just trying to survive.

Yes, the privilege of a white woman
but what as the daughter
of a woman in the asylum?
Who knows where whose madness

comes from or goes?
Iron beds and iron bars.
Copper cans turning green
in the crematorium

a lone headstone
among nameless concrete slabs
reclaimed by family a century later.
This story, too, these.

But, not so pure as the really righteous.
Poor people with aberrant genes
not hated, just don't come near.
Even the psychiatrist said, *Don't marry one.*

BOUNTIES

Bounty beyond bounties
gift boxes with nuts
pecan, pistachio, walnut
cashew, bounty I never saw
until my father died
and fresh strawberries.

He was ill for a long time
but, would you kill your father
for this? Nuts!

Hazel nuts, *noisette*.
We used to call them filberts.
How special, gift box
gift wrapped, and they
kept coming and coming.

My Father's Wine Glasses
for Beverly

My father's three wine glasses.
Are they 'important'? No, not at all.
After all, glass is just sand.

And, they're a bit squat, as was he.
Old, yes, and he, if he'd lived
now older than possible.

But, the memories are important. (Are they?)
How is it that an object, or objects
can be the keepers of memory?

He drank very little, (the glasses are small)
a little 'Haute Sauterne' that came from a jug
when such things first became American.

He offered some to our elegant middle school teacher
who, amazingly, came to a party around the piano.
(I wonder for the first time in many decades
what ever happened to her.)

He didn't drink much, but was an actor and taught me
when portraying someone who's drunk
a big mistake is to be too sloppy.
One tries to maintain, if excessively, dignity.

Now they're kept on a shelf
in a nice cabinet, without fanfare.
Of the three, one is chipped.
Is that important?

Once in a while I take them out
for a special occasion, such as
moving to a new place, a little one
for old age, the last, perhaps.

And, we toast with a splash
(which is all they hold)
feeling it has meaning, and wonder how
the object can possibly hold the memory

but it does, this glass that is just sand.

1950's

My father
liked newish things.
He was all over
Velveeta and Spam.
(After all, this was the 50's.)
He tried chicory coffee.
Why? I'll have to reach
for the history books.

And, he liked inventing things
not big things, not with
the gravity (or talent) of a scientist
but, lightheartedly.

I remember a peppermint cigarette
inspired by a fondness
for dipping the filtered end
in his coffee —

Tiny pouches of extract
sealed in saran wrap
(still the 50's you know)

implanted in the filters
with the care of a surgeon
to be pinched before smoking.

Someone actually marketed
something like that
decades later.

An actor, he liked
speaking in phony accents
impersonating imaginary persons
a character with character.

He liked
singing to me
at night, a song he made up —
*into two too pretty blue eyes
a grain of sand must fall —*
before my eyes turned green.

He was jovial and kind.
He liked many things.

He liked cooking
"with every pot in the kitchen"
according to my snooty, long
dead aunt: meatballs and goulash

and Romanian eggplant
chocolate cake from a mix
(the indomitable 50's)
char burgers like small footballs.

He liked
the tiniest glass
of lowbrow wine

and played a chef
on the radio
in full regalia.

He liked many things.
He was kind. He lost
his memory, his mind.

I'm old enough
to lose my own now
but it's loyal and nurturing
if unreliable.

My language is simple
because I was young.
He would have been
a hundred and ten
next year.

I speak with a sudden
overwhelming longing
to remember everything
about him

the filament of meaning
that belongs to him

more alive, perhaps
than when he was alive.
Children aren't able
to mourn. More alive
than half a century
of silent, insensate grief.

My words are plain
because he died too young.
No other language can convey
the wing-tipped cheer.

Why the Old Look Backwards
In Memoriam: Bob Malison and Tamara Razi

It's not that sentiment
becomes more palpable
or time tenderizes.

But, that so much was missed
ignored as it was happening
although quietly encoded, *sotto voce*
in the tundra of memory —

the voice and gestures of someone
you might not have thought of in years
their belonging in the circle drawn
around the fire of belonging.

Someone younger, and kinder.
Not love, exactly, not dailiness
memoir or award
but being.

Our irrepressible
love of being.

A lifetime happens
long or short.
A lifetime is an aliquot
a box

hours like fingers
touching the forgotten
ridges of memory
words that mean
what it means
 to be.

V

V

Persona Poem

I was born
during the war.

My parents welcomed me
quickly, and briefly
as time might be short.

I was born during the war.
I was born.

I made it to now
dirty and hungry
a bit hollow-eyed
for the well-heeled camera.

I made it through
to now, with dirty arms
still a child's smile
some days
for an opulent lens.

I think of a safe place.
Where can that be?

There are so many of us, throngs.
Where have we come from?
We were born.

You wonder
how did we get here?
We were born.
We were born.

Over and over
we were born
like stars
obliterating the sky.

The goal of life
is not happiness. No
happiness is always here.
The goal is
to suffer less.

In The Catacombs

So many bones
repetitive and decorative
symbolic in so many iterations
but of what?

Once conscious millions
now without light.

So many souls, once.
They're gone now, and I am not.
How do you make sense of that?

Once upon a time in normal graves
the calcified ghosts slyly floated up
only to be reinstalled, osseous arms
and skulls alike, in this popular place.

More beneath Paris than dancing above.
They check your bags not
for terrorism, but grave robbing.

You can't steal, but can
become them. I'm alive and
breathing the conundrum.

The skullduggery of it all!

Having inherited something
of my father's theatricality
I once asked a friend
"What is the meaning of life?"

She replied seriously
None, but what we give it.

They're gone now, centuries
of venerable Parisians
and I am not
yet.

FOR EMILY STOVER (1967-2020)
Emily, you ornament the earth...
— Laura Nyro

Fuck those poems to the living.
They don't need them, they're alive.
And, what good those to the dead?

But, being left with nothing
but words is lonely. Where are you
in the universe I've searched?

It was not unexpected.
Returning to family thin as glass
smiling still, I don't know how

so many years beyond bad news.
Watching the puppy everyone thought
you were crazy to get become an old dog

(Who has the dog?)

Thin as paper (how we hated being fat)
and sleepy. Never mind the family
this and thats, the ex everyone thought
should have done better.

I'm lonely for you this very moment
watching cows graze on a hillside
wondering why do they all line up
in the same direction?

It was not unexpected. You did not
unexpect it. Not by years beyond.

Why do a surfeit of moods line up
as if there's order in the universe
to contemplate a half forgotten Proustian
aunt who spent her life dying?

When she did, half thought her vindicated
and half believed morbid anticipation
had killed her. Your antithesis absolute.

Not not not unexpected but now
now gone. I won't repeat a certain kind
of incomprehensible knowledge
infallible, too, too, religious, just that

you managed to live a very long time.

And, though I do not celebrate bravery
for playing or not playing "the cancer card"
you refused to play. I celebrate your refusal
to sit in death's waiting room like

anyone else we might have known
waiting for death as forecast until
it became time to sleep a lot.

If there's anything I've learned
I've learned, *You die as you've lived*
and, *You live 'til you die.*

Hospital Sport

In the hospital room
in the next bed over
veiled by a thin veil
there seems to be football
on TV. *Yuck!* I'd rather see
a *murder and mayhem*
(as my husband would say)
rerun.

The young man behind the curtain
who arrived 2nd doesn't have
my husband's spectacular view
of the harbor, bridges, and boats
that happen to be frozen in place
by winter, the fine artistry
of ice. Yes, I mean
truly spectacular.

I don't much get sports
but my father played football
nearly a century ago for Wisconsin
or was it the famed Michigan
so long ago they weren't famed?

As I recall, now from the view
of old age, he fractured his elbow
in a rough game. They said
it would be frozen in flexion forever
(which would allow him to touch
his face, and shave). But, something
got better, and by the time
I was born he had a normal arm
albeit shorter than the other.

I remember this story
with all poignancy attributable
to memory. But still, with apology
and some embarrassment
I find sports as alien as God.

Why do hospital architects
think double rooms are a good idea
having given up World War infirmaries —
doctors going down the isle stroking feet
for signs of life, or Babinskis?

A restaurateur I knew offered
hospitality is a Latin sibling of *hospital*.
Hospes — *hospice, hostel, hotel*
the picturesque solace of being
cared for as a guest or stranger
if not too uncomfortable
if not too infirm.

Through the thin shield between us
it sounds like the nice young man
who by nature or nurture
loves those damn sports
doesn't have a grave prognosis
either, thankfully, thank you
this time.

It's Not Death

It's not death that frightens me
the rigmarole, or even the threat
of pain. There's stuff for that.
It's the goodbye.

Oh, I'm not always happy, or never
only happy. Who is? Who can possibly be
amidst this history? Or, nature
was never quite so kind.

But, light enters with the breeze
fluttering the diaphanous curtains
moving like a transparent sea
the light of mind, shadowy as it may be.

Corporeal with imagination, or the lack
I love every hour, however wasted, every distraction.
I love every blistered, apocryphal moment.
As tho' to breathe were life!

The C Word

No, not me, *sigh*
a literary sigh of relief.
But, will it be? When
will it be my turn?

Or, precocious in worry
should I write in advance
So, now it's my turn in the great
turning of the great

wheel of fortune
or mis-? Or, is it merely
a Ferris wheel with flags
ups and downs, downs and ups

sometimes getting stuck or
rarely, toppling? *Enough!*

C is for *Cancer*, a curse word
and a curse. Why are so many
courted, or threatened
breaching the body inviolate?

I can imagine myself lying there
being cared for in that antiseptic way
the tedium of reciting my name
and birthday, again and again

while the bracelet is read.
I can imagine being lonely
or scared, tired but breathing
tired of breathing.

The two things I'm most scared of
aside from being a widow
are cancer and dementia
though if the latter comes first

Welcome Cancer!

Why did 2 favorite cats
die of it before they had a decade?
And, the one I didn't love — yes
there are cats I don't love — made it to 23?

"How long am going to have to
uh, put up with her?" I asked
the vet when she was about 17
all in good humor, of course.

Everyone laughed except the vet
who only smiled, awkwardly.
She wasn't a *bad* cat — friendly enough
very pretty — just sort of dull, and entitled.

RIP Marmalade.

Does loss hurt less if you stop
counting the particulars, let it slosh
as one big, amalgamated
pool of sorrow

that can be stepped away from
into the sun, sometimes, to squeal
with enthusiasm, and ride the Ferris
wheel of fortune?

Please don't say
I fought a courageous battle
any battle at all. What
choice is there? Just say

"She *died*."

The End of Immortality

> *Dying is a part of life, a very important part,*
> *and it's worth doing with some grace.*
> — Elise Snyder

You have a life span
like a wing span
only one.

Some are short
and some are long —
swan and sparrow

Not pre-ordained
but the longest
can never be made longer.

(The longest is an albatross.)

A singular span, hard
to grasp, hard to think
it's ever enough.

Impossible to say, *wait*
there's something I forgot.
Why didn't I learn to dance?

Something more graceful
another window
of forgiveness. Courage

perhaps.

This is the last time
I'm going to write
on this tired subject.

I promise. Pay attention!

You do your day
you do your wings
I'll love you still

absent as breath
leaving the station
ever to me.

Where do the memories go?
I'll hold them
as long as I can.

Arc

What is it that
makes us lean, sway
human or tree —
dance or gravity?

A theme here — the way
she leaned on her death bed
a stroke perhaps, a last gesture
of artistry. Lean, perhaps

to bow with the wind, say
there was motion, always
motion, to say there was
graceful repose, if not grace.

To say to say
the arc of a willow
or an oak. A rainbow?
Unrepentant

for sentimentality.
Unrepentant for arcing
to bear the weight
of humility.

NOTES

You May Want, page 5
line 20, *till they showed the banjo strings*, Robert Frost, "Wild Grapes", 1920.
line 32, *What are those fuzzy looking things out there?* W.C. Williams, "The Last Words of My English Grandmother", 1924.
line 39, *Nothing will come of nothing*, Shakespeare, *King Lear*, Act I, Scene 1.

Ephemera, page 7
line 8, *et tu Brute?* Shakespeare, *Julius Caesar*, Act III, Scene 1.

Generational, page 11
line 1, *All I really want to do, is, baby*, "All I Really Want to Do", Bob Dylan, 1964.
line 18, *Clay and wattles*, W.B. Yeats, "The Lake Isle of Innisfree", 1888.

Keeping the Dead Alive, page 30
line 18, *After great pain*, Emily Dickinson, 372, 1862.

The Grievous Body, page 37
epigraph – *This is thy hour O soul, thy free flight into the wordless...* and section 4, line 4, "A Clear Midnight", Walt Whitman, 1892.
section 1, line 27, *loved the sorrows of your changing face*, W.B. Yeats, "When You Are Old", 1893.
section 7, line 10, *respite of breath*, John Ford, *The Broken Heart*, 1633.

for **Emily Stover**, page 75
9th & 10th stanzas, allusion to Aunt Léonie, Marcel Proust, *Remembrance of Things Past, Volume I, Swann's Way*, 1913.

It's Not Death, page 79
line 16, *As tho' to breathe were life*, A.L Tennyson, "Ulysses", 1833.

LAURI ROBERTSON has written poetry for many years–Adrienne Rich was her mentor. Her first book, *An Æsthetic of Stone,* was published by Spuyten Duyvil last year. Two new pre-2020 volumes, *Where Do the Memories Go?* and *In Concert,* are now offered in tandem. Lauri is a psychiatrist/psychoanalyst formerly on the clinical faculty of Yale Medical School. She's also a fine art photographer, represented on Nantucket Island by The Gallery at Four India: laurirobertsonphotography.com

www.ingramcontent.com/pod-product-compliance
Lightning Source LLC
Chambersburg PA
CBHW012007120526
44592CB00040B/2653